Thinking Like a Writer

A handy guide guaranteed to inspire you!

BY LOU WILLETT STANEK

RANDOM HOUSE NEW YORK

I am fortunate to have enough captivating cousins to fill Yankee Stadium. This is dedicated to them, especially to the younger ones, who with a little luck might become writers: Mitch Arnold, Ben Arnold, Jim Atteberry, and Amy Fuqua.

All rights reserved under International and Pan-American Copyright Conventions. Published in the United States by Random House, Inc., New York, and simultaneously in Canada by Random House of Canada Limited, Toronto.

© *The Thinker*, Auguste Rodin, the Rodin Museum, Philadelphia: Gift of Jules E. Mastebaum

Library of Congress Cataloging-in-Publication Data
Stanek, Lou Willett.
Thinking like a writer / by Lou Willett Stanek.
p. cm.
ISBN 0-679-86217-X (pbk.) ISBN 0-679-96217-4 (lib. bdg.)
1. Creative writing (Elementary education) 2. Children's writing.
I. Title.
LB1576.S752   1994
372.6'23—dc20   93-43966

Manufactured in the United States of America

10 9 8 7 6 5 4 3 2 1

Contents

PART ONE

Thinking Like a Writer

The Notebook

You learn to write by writing. Trust me. Steffi Graf was not born the world's best women's tennis player. Sting did not leave his birth hospital singing "Show Me the Way to Go Home," and, I swear, Shakespeare penned some pretty silly stuff before he wrote *Romeo and Juliet*.

Of course you want to improve your writing. Even if you're planning to play lead guitar with a rock band or be a marine biologist, you will want to write letters people will bind with blue ribbons to keep forever, or preserve special memories in a journal. Imagine being grown up and not able to remember your best friend in fifth grade or the color of your favorite cat. Memories like the first time you danced with a boy or kissed a girl are surely meant to be saved.

Before you read another word, buy a notebook to fit in your pocket.

Now the fun begins.

The unbreakable rules are:

• **Keep the notebook on your person *always*.** I recommend checking the size of pockets before picking pajamas. Some of your best ideas will pop into your mind when you are in bed, or in the shower. Unfortunately, I've never been able to find a waterproof notebook.

• **Writers don't miss anything.** They notice the smell of cookies in the oven, the color of grape jelly, the wacky way a dachshund walks, the look on a snooty kid's face. They eavesdrop. They know that people say the weirdest things when they're in an elevator or on the bus, when they're dressing for gym or having a soda with a girl they have a crush on. A rainy Sunday afternoon is not so boring when you try to describe how a raindrop feels on your eyelid or the pattern it makes on a window.

• **Write down everything.** What you see, taste, touch, hear, smell, and feel should go in the notebook. It's material. Where did teacher and author Jon Scieszka find his idea for *The True Story of the Three Little Pigs*? He says the ideas in his notebook came from listening to the goofiest of second graders. That's really what he said—I read it in a magazine. Norma Mazer has kept a notebook since she was your age. Notes about the person who became the basis for the character Kara in *Out of Control* had been in her notebook for years.

What Do I Put in My Notebook, Anyway?

Divide your notebook into sections. Reserve a place for character names, another for words you like, and certainly a place for feelings. As you begin to think like a writer you will add more sections that have special meaning for you.

Names

Let's begin with nifty names you might use for characters. Newspapers, magazines, movies, soap operas, the family Bible, and talkative seatmates on public transportation are all good sources. Sometimes just names and nicknames like Johnny Bob, Tanner, Princess, Spook, Mary Elizabeth, Chip, Heather, Ruthie, Jake, Juan, Butch, Carmen, Herbert, May Ling, Slugger, Cheyenne, Peewee, or Ashley will suggest a character you could put in a story.

Don't forget to collect names for animals. A racehorse named Dobbin would surely have an inferiority complex, and how could a fat basset hound ever live up to the name Socrates?

Did anyone ever give you a nickname you hated?

Get rid of it! Create an unpleasant character in a story and give it to him or her.

EXERCISES

1. If you could give yourself a new name, it would be...
2. Five appropriate names for a haughty girl are...
3. The best-looking boy in school should be named...
4. A good name for a mean, scary person would be...
5. A father who adores his daughter might give her the pet name...
6. If you could launch a spaceship, it would have the name...written on its nose.
7. A blue-ribbon name for a gerbil would be...
8. If you were going to make up the name of a town, you would call it...
9. A favorite uncle could be called..., but one who embarrasses or ignores you would be named...
10. You can buy Wavy Gravy and Cherry Garcia ice cream. If you could create a new flavor, what would you call it?
11. Pretend you have designed new dolls to compete with Barbie and Ken. You call them...
12. Pretend you are writing a story with the follow-

ing characters. Choose a fitting name for:
- a lazy monster
- a baseball pitcher
- a school principal
- a rapper
- a unicorn
- a cowgirl
- a nerd
- a computer whiz
- a grouchy grandfather
- a spoiled brat
- a bucking bronco
- a nearsighted doctor

Words
Writers collect and trade words as others do marbles. Reserve several pages in your notebook for funny words like *knickers, flibbertigibbet, dumpling*; beautiful ones like *twilight, gossamer, lilac*; scary ones like *screech, stomp, slice, slimy*; ugly ones like *wart, weasel, sleazy, spit, kraut, knuckle*; and impressive ones like *precise, pernicious, pugnacious*. If you find words you've never seen, look them up in a dictionary. It's like finding a new friend.

You make candy out of sugar, burgers out of beef. Sugar and beef cost money. You use them up. In comparison finding the ingredients for your stories is a snap. Words are free, the supply is unlimited, and they don't spoil or attract ants.

Rich or poor; black, brown, white, pink, red, or yellow; young or grown up; top or bottom of the class—you can have as many words as you want. All you have to do is look and listen, and soon you will have a notebook filled with treasures. Like *bubble*.

What things bubble? What color is a soap bubble? A bubble is beautiful, but there's something sad about it too. How long does it last? Why do little kids always want to pop bubbles? Would you describe a bubble as fragile, frail, feeble, delicate? Some kids wear rings that look as if a bubble landed on their finger. I once saw a sheep whose wool made him look as if he were wearing a bubble bath. What else looks like bubbles? Pots that bubble over make a dreadful mess; feelings that bubble over can get on people's nerves. I think there might be a story or at least a poem in a bubble.

Writers select their words as carefully as they do their clothes. You wouldn't wear your jeans to the White House, and you wouldn't call the queen of England cute. Picking the right word to make the proper impression takes some thought. For example, *trash* (even though it might contain just as many rotten orange rinds) has more class than *garbage*. Let's say you're writing a story about your boyfriend and the baby you sometimes sit for. Which of the following words would you use to describe your boyfriend, and which would you save for the baby: adorable, appealing, cute, charming, darling, precious, pretty, lovable? I'd have a replacement picked out before I called a guy precious.

EXERCISES

1. Make a list of words that stink.
2. Find five words to describe a snowstorm.
3. Think of words that sound like what they mean, such as *swirl* or *swish*.
4. Discover verbs that create a picture, like *wiggle, roar, jab.*
5. Make a list of words to define friendship.
6. Think of six words that make you giggle.
7. A kiss is like…; …; …; …; …
8. The ten words that best describe you are:
9. Swipe all the words you never want to be called, like *jerk*. Lock them in your notebook, only to be used when you want one of your characters to hurt someone's feelings.
10. What sounds do the machines in your house make? Think about the refrigerator, the washing machine, the telephone.
11. When you hear a noise in the middle of the

night, which word best describes how you feel? Afraid, scared, anxious, fearful, petrified, terrified, horrified?

12. Hold a contest with a friend to see who can find more of the following:
    • the most disgusting word of the day
    • the longest word
    • the scariest word of the day
    • the weirdest use of a verb on the sports page
    • a poetic word
    • words of endearment, like *cutie, sweetie, sweetpea, honeybun*

Making New Things Out of Old Words

Figurative Language

Did you ever make a puppet out of an old sock? You've seen artists who make pieces of art out of water pipes, automobile tires, pieces of string, or soda pop bottles. Writers use everyday words to create unusual word pictures; my friend Leslie wrote a poem called "Summertime Is Ripe." *Figurative language* is a literary term that means using familiar words in unfamiliar ways.

Let's take some ordinary words and have some fun making them strut their stuff. We'll make figures of speech out of common words. This is like taking a plain white sheet cake, cutting it in two pieces, putting jam between the layers, and adding lemon frosting, coconut, candied cherries, and candles to make a birthday cake. I might have added too much to that cake. Do you think it could be too sweet? Writers have to be careful to include enough details to give a clear picture but not to overdo until the result is cluttered or unappealing.

The same rule applies to using figures of speech. Employed sparingly they add interest. Overused they have the same effect as makeup applied with a heavy hand, or too many baseball patches on your jacket.

Alliteration

Let's begin with a kind of figurative language that is easiest to recognize and to create: *alliteration*. Alliteration is the repetition of initial identical consonant sounds. For example, a cute, cuddly kitten; Sally sings soprano; don't drag the dog; a galloping galoot; a boy brought bagels; whirling wheels. Vowel sounds can be alliterative too: "Apt alliteration's artful aid is often an occasional ornament in prose."

Alliterative people names, like Maniac Magee, can be funny.

EXERCISE

Use the following in an alliterative phrase or sentence:
- soapy
- night

- pimple
- baby
- dimple
- zany

Simile

If you've ever said something like "Taking care of my little brother is as bad as going to the dentist," you already know how to create a *simile*, a figure of speech that makes a comparison by using the words *like* or *as*. By making a clever correlation, you use a simile to clarify an idea or an image. For example, you could say "The dungeon is as dark as a moonless night," or "My dog looks like a Polish sausage on legs," or "His plan was as empty as a church on Monday." But similes have to make sense. If you said "hot as ice" or "She was pretty as the pope," the reader would think you're nuts. You also wouldn't want to say "hot as fire" or "pretty as a picture" because those expressions are clichés, a sure sign of a lazy writer, which you are not. If you can't think of a fresh comparison, it's best simply to say "The soup is hot" or "She is pretty."

Metaphor

A *metaphor*, like a simile, makes comparisons, but without using the words *like* or *as*. The similarity is implied, as in "My dog is a dope"; "Black is beautiful"; "Love is red"; or "When they were giving out brothers, I got the booby prize." Similes are easier to invent, but metaphors usually pack more punch.

Good metaphors make you stop to think; for example, a mother said, "Sending my child off to kindergarten had the thrills and excitement of launching a rocket."

EXERCISE

Create a metaphor or a simile to make an interesting comparison for the following:
- my bike
- fried chicken
- my boyfriend
- baby-sitting
- my grandmother
- our car
- having a tooth filled
- homework
- learning to dance
- thunder
- raw eggs
- a lazy cat

Personification
Personification is a figure of speech that endows animals, ideas, abstractions, or inanimate objects with human form, character, or sensibilities. It represents

something as having human personality, intelligence, and emotions. For example, "My dog is a Democrat"; "The sun flirted with me"; "Education can strike at any time"; "My oldest pair of jeans is my best friend." You can use personification to add color or interest to letters, essays, and other nonfiction. But fiction writers create entire stories about animals who think, speak, and get into as much trouble as we do. Anthony Browne's *Willy the Wimp* (about a chimp) and Richard Adams's *Watership Down* (about a whole bunch of rabbits) are good examples.

EXERCISES

1. Personify your school building, your skateboard, or the dust balls under your bed.
2. Personify your shoe, which insists upon eating your sock.
3. Identify what is personified in the following sentences:
   • Joy deserted me.
   • My goldfish's mother should have taught him not to stare.
   • The little white cloud cried.

Oxymoron
Just saying the word *oxymoron* has to make you giggle.

Being able to spell it has to make you feel clever. Being able to create one is even more fun. This figure of speech brings together two contradictory terms, like "modern classic," "loud silence," "honest lie," "blind sighted," and, the best of all, "happy ending." Shakespeare and other poets were especially fond of oxymorons.

EXERCISES

1. Identify the oxymorons in the following:
   • Parting is such sweet sorrow.
   • The best of the cutthroats.
   • Our house is a grand ruin.
2. Create an oxymoron to use in your work.

Irony

Irony is the most sophisticated figure of speech and is not to be confused with sarcasm, its harsher, meaner cousin. An ironic statement is one in which the author or character says one thing but actually means the opposite: "Your leaving grieves me" says your hero to a bratty cousin whose visit has ruined his life for a week. Ironic words of praise imply blame: "What would I do without you?" says a character to a little sister who has ruined her new lipstick scrawling on the bathroom mirror.

Sarcasm is a form of verbal irony that pretends to praise, but actually is caustic, bitter, and expresses strong personal disapproval. Irony is light and witty. Sarcasm, a sneering taunt, is intended to hurt. For example, if you were creating an unsympathetic coach, when a boy strikes out, the coach might say to the sad kid, "John, you're a star headed for the majors, no doubt about it."

When you write stories you will want to understand dramatic irony, a device in which the reader knows more than the character. The best-known example is when Huckleberry Finn decides not to turn in Jim, the runaway slave. Huck says he knows he is wicked and will go to hell, but he just can't rat on Jim, while the reader knows Huck's impulses are pure.

EXERCISES

1. Write an ironical response you could make to the following situations (if you're creating a mean-minded character, write a sarcastic response):
   • On Friday afternoon you receive homework that will take all weekend to finish.
   • Someone who is wearing an ugly dress asks you how she looks.
   • For your birthday, your brother gives you jeans three sizes too large.

2. Use dramatic irony to create the following situations:
   • You know your parents have planned a surprise birthday party for your sister.
   • On your way home from school, you saw your friend's dog get hit by a car.

Pun

The most playful figure of speech, the *pun* is a humorous play on words that are identical or similar in sound but have different meanings: "The sun is up, but not my son," for example. The use of a single word or phrase with two incongruous meanings, such as *puff* (the verb and the noun), can also make a pun.

Puns can drive perfectly sane people to the loony bin, but they are hard to resist; even Shakespeare couldn't refrain. Charles Lamb said that a pun is a pistol let off at the ear, not a feather to tickle the intellect. However, puns *can* make you laugh. Here's one from M. E. Kerr's *Little, Little:* "There's no place like Gnome."

However, puns, like all figures of speech, should be used cautiously. When writing dialogue, give your puns to the wackiest, most wisecracking character.

Figurative language is most effective when it is rare and unexpected. If you can't think of a unique comparison or a really funny pun, skip it. Sprinkle figures of speech lightly through your work, in the same way you would apply a good perfume.

EXERCISES

1. Make a pun out of pop.
2. Invent a red pun.
3. Create a pun out of corn.

Feelings

Writers write about what they like; what they hate; what scares them, fascinates them, embarrasses them, and makes them happy. So can you. They write about what others do, say, and feel, like what your dad said when you poured orange pop on your brother's head, or what your sister said when she found you behind the couch when she was entertaining a boy. Terrific ideas are swirling all around you, just waiting for you to grab them. I suggest having sections in your notebook for the following:

- Things I Would Like to Know More About
- Things That Surprise Me
- Things I Want to Accomplish This Year
- Things I Daydream About
- The Funniest Thing I Saw Today
- The Saddest Thing I Noticed Today
- What Scares Me

- What Makes Me Angry
- Places I Would Most Like to See
- How I Feel When I Hear My Favorite Music
- My Favorite Books
- The Best Things About My Family
- The Worst Things About My Family

Finding Things to Write About

You have a unique life. No one else feels as you do, or sees things in exactly the same way. Find the words to welcome readers to your world. Successful writers suggest you really *see* the faces of people in the streets. Ask yourself questions about strangers you pass: the man who regularly talks to his dog as he walks, but never speaks to people. Why does he do that? The sad little boy who sits on his porch and never waves back. What makes him so sad? What is it about his face that leads you to believe he is unhappy? Why does that older boy on the block scare you, even though he has never said a word?

Pretend you are a camera. Your notebook becomes your word-picture album. Coming to school, even on a raw Monday morning, can be an adventure when you are looking for sights to put in your notebook, like the boy on the subway who looks as if he dunked his hair in orange Kool-Aid. Or how about the yard where the mean dog snarls as you pass? Then there is the hunk-of-a-guy working at the candy store, who seems to notice you every morning. Don't forget the car license plate that says I AM LATE, or the T-shirt that says IF YOU DON'T THINK YOU CAN BUY HAPPINESS, YOU DON'T KNOW WHERE TO SHOP.

Don't miss things in your house or your friends' homes. I recently visited someone who had upholstered a chair in fabric that felt like sandpaper. It made me itch. He called himself Daddy to his cat. That made me itch the most. I'll use it in a story someday.

Cushions on chairs in doctors' offices can make an embarrassing sound when you sit down, and they stick to your legs if you're wearing shorts. The greengrocer in my neighborhood lines up pieces of fruit as if they were sitting on the bleachers at the ballpark. His nectarines wear rouge; the peaches only blush. I know a man who wears pink sneakers. It's okay if you want to use any of these ideas in your stories, but don't overlook the weird, interesting things on your own block.

If you're afraid your brothers and sisters will think you're giving away secrets if you write about them, a cousin can be a good source. If she lives out of town, she won't even know you told about the corny note she wrote to the college boy who mows the lawn...until you're published. And by that time she'll probably have forgotten all about him.

Did you ever notice the bizarre things men do when they begin to lose their hair, like letting the sides grow long and flopping the hair over the top? You could write a funny story about what happens to a man's hairdo in a wild and woolly windstorm. I know a man who is bald on top but has long flowing locks growing all around, like fringe on a bowling ball. Would you describe these hairstyles as weird, eccentric, odd, peculiar, strange, ingenious, clever, canny, creative, artful?

I once had a horse that laughed at me. Honest. He curled back his lips and showed his teeth. They were as big as dominoes and almost as black. One summer in Maine a mean-minded sea gull got it in for me. He sat on my deck and yelled at me for almost a whole day. Have you ever had an encounter of a strange kind with an animal? Write about it. Look at what E. B. White did with a spider named Charlotte.

Above all don't forget your fantasies. Alex Alexiou is thirteen, lives in Bellmore, New York, and goes to school as you do. But in the stories he writes, he has daring adventures like saving damsels in distress and making the Baseball Hall of Fame before he is old enough to vote. In one story Alex wrote, he and two teenage buddies ran the A&B Detective Agency. When a girl their age was kidnapped, they relied on crafty logic to find the girl, solve the case, and even impress the local police with their shrewdness. To make the Baseball Hall of Fame at a tender age, Alex simply created a story about a professional Little League baseball division. Why not?

It doesn't matter if you live on a farm or in a small town, in the suburbs or the city, in a mansion or the projects. People will want to read about it, if you can find the words to let them see the picture.

Turn your eyes into a camera lens looking for a good shot. Sometimes you'll see it outside your front door, sometimes in your imagination. See what you can do with the following:

EXERCISES

1. The first thing I see when I wake up is…
2. I have a secret place…
3. The scariest place I've ever been is…
4. My feet look like…
5. At a store in my neighborhood, what caught my eye was…
6. At my home our most prized possession is…
7. If I were an artist in my town, I would paint…
8. My favorite outfit is…
9. I once saw a… I wanted it so much that I can still remember it; it was…
10. The most hideous thing I ever had to wear was…

11. My closet looks like…
12. One day in the park I watched…
13. When I want to be alone at home, I go…
14. If a foreign exchange student came to stay with my family, I think she would be impressed by…
15. I've seen people make interesting jewelry out of…
16. The funniest message I ever saw on a T-shirt said…

Here are some exercises about people and animals.

EXERCISES

1. If I were casting a movie, I would have my friend…play the role of a…because he has…
2. The first thing you notice about my mother is…
3. The nicest person on our block is… He…
4. The ugliest animal I ever saw was…
5. My boyfriend's/girlfriend's best feature is…
6. …'s hands intrigue me because they are…
7. … is my idol because…
8. If I could hug a porpoise, I think he would feel like a…
9. If I could have any pet I wanted, I would choose a…

10. The most unpleasant clerk I've ever dealt with in a store was…because she made me feel…
11. Once I had a teacher who…
12. You could recognize our mail carrier in a crowd because…

Descriptive Details

Would you rather have ice cream, or chocolate ice cream with swirls of peanut butter, chunks of cashew nuts, and bits of white chocolate?

Which of the following pen pal letters would you answer? "My name is Charles. I am twelve. I like to play baseball." Or "Mom named me Charles, which I think is a stupid name to call someone who is going to be a Hall of Fame pitcher for the Cardinals. My curve ball can cross a batter's eyes. At twelve, I'm five feet five inches tall, but I don't plan to stop growing until I'm six feet three."

Create a picture in your mind of a bike. What happens when I tell you it's rusty? Or it's rusty now, but once it was pink? Or it's a rusty boy's bike that once was pink? Or it's a boy's bike, once pink but now rusty, with a child's seat attached?

Pretend you're dressing for school. Your shirt is

clean. What will look nice with it? Oh, I forgot to tell you it's an oversize blue turtleneck. Does that make a difference?

Here is what sets apart writers like you. Anyone can see a picture in her mind; writers like you find the words to create the picture so that others can see it too. Imagine a balloon. What color is yours? Has it been blown up, or is it lying limp in your hand? Is it long? Round? Does it have ears? How big is it? Is anything printed on it? It's the small details that really bring the picture into focus. Mark Twain said that the difference between the right and the not-so-right word is like the difference between lightning and a lightning bug.

A man with a bump on his nose is more interesting to read about than one whose features you can't see. A shirt that could stand a washing raises interesting questions in a story. *Nice* and *good* are the two most boring, boring, boring ways to describe anything. What does "He was a nice man" or "She was a good girl" tell you? I'd rather read about the bump on his nose or her dirty blouse.

Look at your shoes. If all the students in your classroom took off their shoes, and the teacher piled them up, how would you describe yours so that I could find them?

I don't know your best friend, but I would like to meet him. Describe him so that I'll recognize him if I see him in the park someday.

Tell me about your room. It's okay to close the closet door, if you didn't get around to cleaning it on Saturday. Describe the furniture. What is on your bed? If you're embarrassed about still having your favorite stuffed animals, leave them out. What's on the walls? Under the bed? Is anything locked? Where do you keep your diary? Your socks?

Blue is my favorite color because it reminds me of the ocean. In my house, everything but the butter is blue. If I came to visit you, could I tell something you especially liked just by looking around your house? I have a room filled with books that used to fit on the shelves, but I think they reproduce themselves at night. They've spilled all over the place. I know someone who fills his shelves not with books but with statues of eagles.

I have a friend who has cat earrings, a cat bracelet, and cat sweatshirts. Her sneakers have cat faces on the toes. I'm not kidding.

There are pigs all over my house. I have a pig cheese board, pig wind chimes, even a pig notepad. It's not that I'm so nuts about pigs, but my nephew Dannon lives in Iowa and he likes playing basketball better than shopping for gifts. So he always sends me pigs. My pig planter is blue—he tries. But Dannon doesn't have pigs all over his room. He has pictures of girls, lots of girls. Whose picture looks at you when you wake up? Do you have any pigs rooting around in your room?

When you are writing a story, you have to create a sense of place and time, so the reader knows where you have taken her. If your story takes place at a school, what details would you give to help her see this particular school? Does she need to know if it's winter or spring? You don't have to state the season; let the reader know by having your characters wear heavy coats, earmuffs, and fuzzy-lined boots that make their feet hot, for example.

If the story is set in your room at home, how could you show it was late at night without actually saying it?

How could you use sounds to create a sense of place? I grew up on a farm. Until I was six years old I saw only one working fire truck. It came out when our haystack started to blaze. I live in New York now. If I don't hear a fire truck siren every few minutes, I think the fire fighters are on strike. Do you hear traffic, birds, people talking next door, or music from down the street?

Okay, let's move on to the hard part—faces. Look in the mirror. Now look at the kid sitting next to you. Eyes, ears, hair, a nose, and a mouth, right? Do you and he look like twins? If you have the same parts, why do you look different?

Hair is easiest, so let's start with it. Color? Clairol has thirteen shades of blond in a bottle. In your school alone there must be twenty-seven other hues. Compare a character's hair to something. Is it more the color of a daffodil, canned corn, wheat, honey, butterscotch, a baby chicken, a Jersey cow? Is the hair long, cropped, braided in cornrows, curly, straight, permed, nappy, thick, stringy, limp, greasy, sprayed, gelled? How much is there? So much it looks as if you'd get tired carrying it around? Would a Dolly Parton wiglet make an improvement? Is it adorned with buttons and bows and clips and combs? Does this character's buzz cut look as if the barber was having a bad day?

Noses are hard, but if you can describe one well that means you're a better writer than most. Is the bridge long? Are the nostrils flared, narrow, or pinched? Does it turn up or spread out? What about freckles? Sunburn? Do the eyes sit close? In profile does the person you're describing look like Caesar or a parrot?

Chins are fun. Some people have too much chin, as if their faces melted and ran down. Others got cheated and have only a little pointy one.

Ears are pretty boring to write about unless they are

big and stick out like hood ornaments.

I once knew someone whose face was as round as a pie. And I don't mean any disrespect for Mr. Lincoln, because he was a brave president, but he did have a face as long as Prince's. Prince was my horse when I was a child.

I like to hear details about character's feet, but I'll leave that to your discretion. Yet, who wouldn't be sympathetic to someone who walked through life with a hammertoe, or a guy whose feet grew faster than his legs and were always getting in the way?

When describing something, don't tell the reader how to feel about it. Let him decide. For example, if you've described someone with a crooked nose, thin lips, snake eyes, and a double chin, you don't have to say he's ugly. If a girl is beautiful, don't say it. Describe her straight teeth, dazzling smile, high cheekbones, and shiny hair. The reader will get it and appreciate your not making the decision for him.

How does a hot dog taste? Would it make your reader hungrier if you added relish and mustard, and toasted the bun? How do baked beans look when you bring the leftovers home from a picnic? What if the little brother in your story scraped the mold off the jelly jar and let your character eat some before he told her? How does it feel to try to swallow peanut butter when it's dried out?

What if your character got out of bed in the middle

of the night and stepped on something mushy? How does a cold soda pop feel on your cheek when it is ninety-seven degrees outside?

The details you choose to describe people, places, and things will make all the difference. You don't need many, just the right one. It's like adding a few sprinkles to your ice cream cone.

You may think first of adjectives like *purple* or *puny*, adverbs such as *swiftly* or *sickly*, nouns like *rapper* or *police officer* to bring your image into focus, but don't overlook the picture power of verbs. An advertiser paid someone a lot of money to dream up "snap, crackle, and pop." Which do you like best—"He yelled" or "He said loudly"? Think about writing a scene where someone is walking. How does the impression change if she skips? If she ambles, saunters, strolls, strides, bounces, or hops, she has not only changed her pace, but demonstrated her mood. The descriptive verb saved you a lot of work.

Verbs can also imply age, education, region, and station in life. Unless your grandmother is friskier than mine, she probably isn't going to hop down the sidewalk. And perish the thought if a princess were to holler. You might carry your books to school, but in Georgia the kids tote theirs.

Writers pay attention to the sound of their verbs too. Why settle for "He was restless" when you can have a character squirm, fidget, wiggle, wriggle, or twist?

EXERCISES

1. Practice finding the right detail for some of the following when you describe:
   - a vegetarian's dinner
   - a windy day
   - a shooter marble
   - a lonely day
   - a cranky mother
   - a thumb
   - a wart
   - a sore toe
   - a stray dog
   - an angry neighbor
   - a boring assignment
   - a sunset
   - a snub
2. What color is:
   - happiness
   - your town
   - defeat
   - Sunday
   - hope
   - a scream

3. How do the following feel:
   - sweaty clothes
   - a mosquito bite
   - a steering wheel
   - an outgrown shoe
   - a baby clutching your finger
   - sand in your sock
   - mud
   - a shower
   - a slap
   - money in your pocket
   - being left out
   - a guilty conscience
4. Rewrite the following, adding details to make the image vivid or easier to picture:
   - The child was lost.
   - The milk was sour.
   - A girl asked me for a date.
   - Michael is overweight.
   - Dad bought a new car.
   - No one liked the new girl.
   - We made a mess.
   - I was ashamed.
   - It embarrassed me to death.
   - My little brother got sick.
   - She forgot again.
   - He cheated.

5. Let's pretend you have created a new product—a soft drink, pizza, a candy bar, lipstick, a line of jeans. Give it a name. Describe it, giving details that would let your customers see it and make them want to buy it.
6. You are sitting on a park bench, minding your own business, when this strange-looking kid joins you and tells you she lives on another planet. Describe what she looks like. Don't forget to tell us what she's wearing.
7. A horse with wings lands in your backyard. You jump on, and he takes you for a ride. Explain how it feels to be riding a horse with a flock of geese or an eagle flying beside you.
8. You have designed a dress to wear to a wedding, a graduation, or a school dance—someplace special. Describe it so a seamstress could picture it.
9. You meet someone who has the weirdest things stored in his computer. Describe what is in there.
10. You find a bug who has learned how to sing. Describe him and how he sounds.
11. It's Halloween, and you want to be a clown. Your mother says you must put together your costume with what you can find around the house. Describe what you use.
12. You built a tree house. Tell where it is, what it

looks like, and how to get up there. You can say who is allowed to visit, if you wish.

13. You open your closet door and find in there someone or something that scares you to death. Describe it.

14. Miraculously, you become a magic genie. Describe what you wear. (You don't have to live in a bottle if it will mess up your harem pants.)

15. Find descriptive verbs to describe:
    - a home run
    - the noise an angry animal makes when he's locked up
    - how it feels on ice skates
    - what a blush does to your face
    - someone's stare when you make a mistake
    - when the parachute opens
    - what a new baby does to peace and quiet in a home
    - a fist hitting you
    - a rock band's lead singer
    - swimming
    - your spirits when you didn't receive an invitation to a party
    - floodwaters

Discovering Different Ways to Write

This book is told from my *point of view* in first person. As I wrote it, I pretended you were right there in my study. I talked directly to you. Before I began, I considered other ways. For example, my personal voice as the author could have disappeared. I could have written something like this:

> "Research has shown writers learn to write by writing. Writing is a skill that requires practice. Repeating exercises helps young writers master the art of writing, just as practicing scales and working out help musicians and athletes."

Who is talking to whom? Reading things that are written from an anonymous viewpoint gives me the creeps. The words read as if they were written by a ghost. It also makes me feel left out, because that ghost certainly isn't talking to me. I feel as if I'm eavesdropping.

Originally, an editor at a different publisher asked me to write this book, but he wanted me to address it to your teachers. That seemed pretty silly, since you were the one who wanted to improve your writing. That book would have been me telling her to tell you. This is the way it would have looked:

> "Students' writing will improve if they practice. Ask your students to do the warm-up exercises that follow. Assure them that writing will become as natural as talking, if they write as much as they speak."

I'm sure your teacher has some terrific ideas to help improve your work, and he will give suggestions, just as I will. All we have done is remove the middleman and ask you to think about the most important decision a writer makes before she puts pencil to paper: From whose viewpoint am I writing, and to what audience? Or, who will be speaking to whom?

I considered another viewpoint for this book. I thought about making up a funny character, giving her a wacky name like Willa Wannabe, and letting her tell you about writing. That book would have sounded like this:

> "Hello, boys and girls. This is Willa Wannabe, writing to you from Walla Walla. Now, I know

all of you want to write like Judy Blume or Stephen King. Well, you can just forget that. You have a voice. Use it. Who wants to hang out with brats like Blume's siblings or do all of those dreadful things to cats anyway?"

That book would have been fun to write, but I was afraid both you and I would get carried away with Willa Wannabe and forget to stick to the business at hand—developing your unique style and voice. Let's start with something like your most embarrassing moment and see how many different ways we can use the same material.

Imagine you are six years old. Your parents are having a party. Everyone you like best and want to impress most is invited—the Little League coach, your grandparents, your favorite kindergarten teacher, even the kid you have a crush on. Trying to help, you light the candles on the table. But...whoops! You set the house on fire, and the fire fighters turn the hose on the table—the one with all the food, wouldn't you know it?

If you were writing a letter to a pen pal, speaking directly and informally, you'd probably describe the incident like this: "Yikes! You won't believe what happened to me when I was only six..."

For a school essay, you would write more formally and remove the slang. You might say, "When I was six, the most humiliating thing happened..."

Now imagine that a reporter from the school paper is interviewing you. "According to Steve Blake, he hasn't always been so cool. The most embarrassing moment in his life happened when he was six and set the house on fire."

And then there's the adult reporter, writing for the local paper: "While lighting party candles last night, six-year-old Steve Blake set the dining room table ablaze in his home at 632 Mulberry Street." (Reporters stick to the facts: who, what, where, when. There is not a sign of the writer's voice in most newspaper journalism.)

Since everything is material for writers like you, Steve could use the incident in a story. But it was embarrassing, right? The fun thing about being a writer is that you can change things around and make up new endings. Steve could create a character, Ben Bumbler. "Ben had a knack for messing up. That's why people called him Ben Bumbler. Why, when he was only six Ben..." Or Steve could have pretended to be Ben writing in first person. "They call me Ben Bumbler. I got that stupid name when I was six and set our house on fire. It was an accident."

Some of you will become novelists writing stories reviewed in *The New York Times*. Others will run large companies and have to write impressive, persuasive letters to your stockholders. As baseball stars and military officers, you will want to write your autobiographies. Movie and rock stars and classical violinists will have to write award acceptance speeches. Computer whizzes, scientists, mathematicians, and economists will have to explain their discoveries. One way or the other, all of you will need to write.

Now that you know you should think about point of view and audience first, *clarity* is next. Being able to say what you mean so others can understand you is very important—it can spell the difference between success or failure.

I know someone who says "You know what I mean?" or "You hear what I'm saying?" ten times a minute. It drives me crazy! Only my mother's insistence on good manners prevents me from screeching, "No! I haven't a clue what you mean. Stop saying that. It's distracting. And it makes me think *you* don't know what you mean either."

If those who use descriptive words like *nice* and *good* or the you-know-what-I-meaners don't drive me daft, the people who write instructions will. If you've ever had directions for a game or a computer program that made no sense, you will understand how important it is to write clear instructions. Let's get started.

We'll practice on something simple. Picture your house, and your street. I'm calling from your school to ask for directions to come to see you. If it's not too far, I'll walk. I'll come by car if it's farther than a mile. How would you direct me?

The key to writing directions is to assume the audience knows nothing. Give essential information in understandable terms in their proper order: "Plug in the computer, switch it on." Do not include any extraneous information. When Dannon moved to Iowa and gave me directions to his new house, he said, "Don't turn off at Exit Six." I said, "Don't tell me how *not* to get there, for pity's sake."

Read recipes. People who write cookbooks usually know how to give instructions in their proper order, like "Preheat the oven to 350 degrees, then sift the flour with the baking soda." Neither Betty Crocker nor the chairman of Apple Computer ever said, "You know what I mean?" Trust me.

EXERCISES

1. Rewrite Steve Blake's embarrassing story from his nerdy cousin's viewpoint as if she were telling a friend. Then write the story from the perspective of the candles on the cake.
2. The score of the football game is tied. It's the last quarter. You're carrying the ball. Your shoelace comes untied. You trip. Write about it

from your point of view, the coach's, or a sports reporter's.

3. What if you are giving your first piano recital? Your sheet music blows off the piano and into the orchestra pit. Write about it from your perspective, your mother's, or your teacher's.

4. What if you want to go to a highly competitive camp (for tennis, cheerleading, computers, dance, or acting) where the slots are limited? Write a letter trying to persuade the administrator to accept you. The trick is to explain your talent or skill without sounding as if you are either bragging or insecure.

5. What if a couple had liked each other for eight months, but now one of them wants to break up? The other one argues that they should stay together. Try writing about it from both points of view.

6. What if a boy is arrested? His father faces the judge. Choose to write about it from the father's or the judge's viewpoint.

7. Write instructions for playing your favorite computer game.

8. Explain how you blow-dry your hair.

9. Write directions for taking public transportation from your house to the mall, a library, or the next town.

10. Write from the viewpoint of a butterfly who spots a kid with a net, or from the viewpoint of a lightning bug who sees someone approaching with a glass jar.
11. Pretend you are a mouse who lives in your school. Write what he thinks of this place. (Make it funny.)
12. In South America llamas are trained to herd sheep. This long-necked animal with his doleful eyes is docile, except when a coyote attacks his herd. Then he trumpets a high-pitched alarm, charges the intruder, and chases, kicks, and paws at it with his front hooves. If the llama is really riled, he will spit. Create a scene in which a coyote sees a lamb as a mouth-watering dinner…until the llama sees him. Write from the viewpoint of either the llama or the coyote. Let's pretend both animals can talk.

Improving Your Writing

It can be okay to look grubby when you're at home, but when you go out you try to look your best; you wash your face, comb your hair, and floss the lettuce out of your teeth. Do the same for your writing. Sometimes ideas flow as fast as raindrops. Before they evaporate, writers scribble them down any which way. After you have captured those thoughts, probably scratched out a few rowdy words, added some details, and maybe moved a couple of phrases around to places where they sound better, there is still another step.

Professional writers call it "cleaning it up." First they clean out the "weasel words." You've probably heard your brother say you're trying to weasel out of helping him rake the leaves, clean the garage, or wash the pots and pans. Weasel words just sit there in your sentences getting a free ride, not doing a lick of work. *That* might be the laziest bum of them all, but *who*, *which*, *all*, and *what* have notorious shiftless reputations also. In the following, the words in parentheses ( ) are clutter:

- Joe, Cindy's boyfriend, (was a kid who) could put a spin on a fastball and her heartstrings.
- (The people that) I would like to introduce you to (are) my cousins Squirt and Peewee.
- (All) I wish (is that) he would give me an A on my test.
- (What I mean to say is that) no one should have to have his teeth drilled.
- (Of all the things in the world which) I can't abide spinach (is the worst).

The poet Wallace Stevens said, "Life is the elimination of what is dead." Eliminate the dead words in your writing.

You're busy. Why take time to use or repeat unnecessary words such as *at the present time* when you mean *now*? Besides, you'll bore your reader silly. Don't say "Suzy is a girl who..." Her name indicates her sex. Why state "Jefferson School is a school I like"? Why write "He called Sam. Sam is his friend," when you can say "He called his friend Sam"?

Redundant means repetitious, superfluous, and unnecessary. For example, if you use a strong verb like *scrutinize*, usually you don't have to qualify it. It is redundant to say "The math teacher scrutinized my paper carefully," since *scrutinize* means to examine carefully. *Habit* means a consistent or frequent action.

"Skip has the habit of consistently turning off his alarm and falling back to sleep"—what is superfluous in that sentence? "She screamed loudly" is perfectly ridiculous; how else can she scream? "He ran fast." Try running slowly!

Overusing a word in your writing can wreck what could have been a humdinger. "Millie has the measles. Measles give you measle spots. Measles itch. Measles look worse than freckles." Why not "Millie's measles gave her itchy spots. They looked worse than freckles"? Rather than repeating a word, use a synonym, a word having the same or nearly the same meaning.

Instead of using *remember* over and over you could substitute the words *recall, recognize, recollect.* If you are writing a story about Harry, don't use poor old Harry's name again and again; break the monotony by using *he* or *the boy* or *that rascal.* Check your work to see if it sounds as if the needle is stuck on one word.

Look for synonyms in a thesaurus, the Latin word for treasure house, in this case a treasure house for words. Writers have been known to call this book their best friend. I have one built into my computer software, and I wouldn't trade it for a yacht. You can buy a paperback thesaurus, or ask the librarian if you may use the school's copy.

Beware of clichés, phrases spoiled by overuse. How many times have you heard "sell like hot cakes," "down but not out," "sadder but wiser," "bitter end," "broad daylight," "cool as a cucumber," "pride and joy"? You don't use other people's toothbrushes. Don't use their words. You're too creative to borrow. Invent your own.

Euphemisms are words that attempt to prettify something distasteful. They are used often to describe bodily functions or scary things such as death, old age, or poverty, but they sound fake. People die; they don't "pass away" or "meet their maker." Saying you are "irregular" doesn't hide a thing. People still know you're constipated. Your report card might say you're "poorly motivated," but your mother knows that means lazy. Calling a slum the "inner city" doesn't make living there any easier. If you are creating a prissy character, let *her* call pus "matter" and old people "senior citizens." For fun, you can have a prudish garbage collector call himself a "waste management engineer."

Passive (inactive, insipid, inert, lifeless) people usually make you yawn. So can passive constructions: "The sting was caused by a bee"; "Joyce was kissed by John"; "Mistakes are sometimes made"; and "The error was brought to my attention." It's more effective to state who did what to whom, in that order: John kissed Joyce; Sue brought the error to my attention. The passive voice suggests nobody is doing anything except sitting around being acted upon. To add zip to your writing, cut those placid passive verbs.

Don't stick an unnecessary preposition on the end of a perfectly good verb. It's like a wart on a nose. Why "kick in" when you can simply "give," or "suit up" for basketball practice instead of "dress"?

If talking about misplaced modifiers sounds like grammar and you are allergic to grammar, put your bias aside. This is different and necessary. A writer needs to know where to put a descriptive phrase, or no one will be able to make sense of what she has written. For example, consider the sentence "Everyone was born in December in this room." Surely, they weren't all born in that room. The writer must mean "Everyone in this room was born in December." The idea is to put the modifier as close as possible to the word it describes or clarifies. Which is better: "He almost understood every word the teacher said" or "He understood almost every word the teacher said"?

One of the quickest ways to make readers lose faith in you is to use a verb that doesn't agree with the subject, such as "he don't" instead of "he doesn't." Another common error is using the wrong case when a pronoun is the object of a preposition ("between you and I" should be rewritten "between you and me"). Using the objective case for a subject doesn't work either. "Me and John are pals" won't make you closer friends; it's "John and I are pals." The double negative is another killer bee—"I don't need no help," when "any help" is correct. It's hard when you hear people speaking incorrectly all around you, even on TV, but writers can't be sloppy. Correctness does matter, a great deal actually. Just as an electrician has to learn which wires to tie together, you as a writer have to learn the proper way to string words together.

But don't despair. Think of all the many things you already know how to do correctly. What you know is amazing. Learning anything is easier when you need the knowledge to apply to a task you want to accomplish. And you want to learn to write as well as Virginia Hamilton, Katherine Ann Paterson, E. B. White, and M. E. Kerr.

I suggest you give your work to someone who knows the rules. When he sees an error, don't just let him fix it—find out why it should be changed. Remember it. Before you know it, you will have patched up the weak spots and will be writing stories to publish in the school paper, or maybe even a magazine.

Have some fun discovering the mistakes in the exercises below.

EXERCISES

1. Willy is a boy who is always in trouble.
2. He lives in a tall skyscraper.
3. My grandmother smiles happily.
4. He slammed the door loudly.
5. As of this date, your paper is due.

6. She dresses along the lines of an actress.
7. My letter is short and sweet.
8. I have to powder my nose.
9. My father passed on.
10. The decision was left up to John.
11. My birthday is in June. On my birthday we go to the zoo, and my granny bakes me a birthday cake.
12. Mom don't care.
13. This secret is to remain between you and I.
14. My dad can't see no team but the Cardinals.
15. He seen it coming.
16. Kim planted a sweet potato for the teacher in a hanging pot.

PART TWO

Writing Fiction

Introduction

When I looked up *fiction* in the thesaurus, I found *story, imagination, invention, fantasy, fabrication, fib.* You can see the big difference between actual personal experience (fact) and fiction (imagined).

Let's say you attend a family picnic in the park. The sun shines. Auntie Sue's fried chicken is as crispy as always. You and your cousins play baseball, and you get three hits. Traffic is light on the way home. The baby sleeps. Your dad sings, and the whole family joins him.

What a pleasant experience. Be sure to put it in your notebook, but, sorry, it's not a story. Now, if it rained, you stepped in the coconut pie, Billy the bully cousin blackened your eye, your dad and his dad had words, Mom's cake fell, and the baby ate some ants—*then* you'd have the makings of a story. Stories have to have *conflict*.

Back to the thesaurus. Synonyms for *conflict* include *trouble, controversy, friction, strife, clash, confrontation.*

Conflict or trouble is what stands between your character and a happy ending. If she doesn't have to struggle for what she wants, it's bound to be a boring story. I'm not saying she can't eventually overcome the problems, but her struggle will create the interest.

Don't get carried away. The conflict doesn't have to be catastrophic. Shootouts, burning buildings, gang wars, car chases, runaway rockets, murky men from Mars, werewolves, man-eating house plants, mad dogs, and monsters with fangs are okay if that's your taste. But the best stories are most often bloodless, about affairs of the heart. Your character's dog dies; her friend moves away; he misses a basket; someone makes her feel foolish; no one chooses him; her dad never married her mother; he begins to like another girl; her mother drinks too much; her parents get a divorce. Or a grandfather loses his memory; a dolphin gets separated from the rest of the herd; a little brat flushes Gilda the goldfish down the toilet, and so begins her journey.

The conflict can be caused by an *antagonist*—a rival, opponent, or sworn enemy. This person stands directly opposed to your main character. You might also think of him as an adversary, an assailant, a foe, a challenger, a competitor, or a contender. All stories don't have to have an antagonist, however. Your character's own nature can cause him more trouble than an enemy. Think what kind of trouble someone's greed could cause her! But when you create a foe, you must understand his motivation as well as your main character's.

If you write about soldiers fighting each other, they may have a philosophical or religious difference. Think of the Civil War or the Arab-Israeli conflict. If your characters play on different teams or are prizefighters, as in Robert Lipsyte's *The Contender*, they're opposing each other for a prize. Stories with abstract conflicts can work well, but some of the best stories pit an individual against another person or thing: Captain Ahab versus Moby Dick, Little Red Riding Hood against the big bad wolf, Cinderella opposed by her wicked stepmother.

The best antagonist (which might be the best oxymoron of the day) is a worthy one. By that I mean he is exceptionally shrewd, clever, intelligent, or strong. Beating him is no easy task. Robert Cormier's *The Chocolate War* has a character who is an extremely worthy antagonist. Archie is not only meaner than a snake, but he is also very good at dirty tricks. All antagonists with evil intent are built on some version of the devil, the prototype of someone who tries to corrupt good. If the devil were a wimp, he would never have been able to lead anyone astray, and we would never have heard of him.

Then there is the worthy opponent who really is worthy. Barbara Kingsolver's *Pigs in Heaven*, an adult story, is about a sensitive, intelligent Native American lawyer who does not feel Indian children should be adopted and raised outside their culture. With honorable intentions, she tries to take Turtle away from a white mother who loves the child as much as Turtle loves her. Neither woman is mean or evil, but only one can win in this situation.

One of the best ways for you to win as a writer is to write the unpredictable. The best tales are not what you expect. Funny stories often grow out of things going haywire. Machines can create trouble. Imagine that a popcorn popper won't stop. When the apartment is full, the popcorn spills out the window until there is a mountain of it. Thousands of people appear and start eating... Or how about an unruly computer that ate your character's history report?

Or nature gets off the track. You character wishes for long hair, and it begins to grow. Scissors won't cut it. It grows and grows and grows until her brothers and sisters have to walk behind her carrying it like a bridal train.

Dependable things can let you down. Your character has to make a speech at the school assembly. Her mom makes her wear a dress. As she walks to the podium, the elastic in her underpants breaks.

Or you can reverse the nature of stock characters. The stepmother is a sweetie pie. The loner becomes your character's best friend. The prince is a nerd.

You ideas are churning. I can hear them. Before they get away, let's find a character who can put them into action.

Creating a Character

This is the fun part!

Some people like to kick balls, kiss boys, make fudge or mischief. People like us like to write stories. Don't misunderstand. It's okay, even preferable, to enjoy all the above and still be an outstanding writer. As a matter of fact, I've always liked to kiss boys, but then I wanted to write about it, and the boys haven't always understood.

Finding a character whose story you want to tell is the starting point. If you have been diligently recording ideas and observations in your notebook, you may already have found someone.

In the beginning, young writers often think it would be easier and more fun to write about themselves, as if they were a character in the story. I suggest you put all of your experiences, feelings, and ideas in the notebook, as we discussed in the first chapter. Use your life experience to write letters, essays, and journals.

Record your memories. Don't lose anything. You learn to write by writing—that's a promise. And you will use all of the material you've been collecting, but now we're going to write fiction, which is a combination of your imagination and your experience. You won't write just about things that really happen. You get to make up things. But it's not fibbing; it's being creative.

At sixteen, S. E. Hinton saw a gang fight in the park. A boy was killed. Using this experience as the core of the story, young Hinton wrote *The Outsiders*. S. E. Hinton happened to be a girl named Suzy. But she didn't write about a girl who saw a gang fight. She created Ponyboy, one of the guys in the gang, and wrote the story from his point of view. That's the difference between experience and fiction.

You've been playing pretend all your life, imagining you were an astronaut, a movie star, a ballerina, a rock star, the chief of your tribe, a major league pitcher, the first woman jockey to ride in the Kentucky Derby. Now you can write your fantasies.

Choose a character you like or would like to know. This is going to be an adventure. You're about to become a method actor. When you've found a character, walk through the world in her shoes. You'll see, taste, touch, smell, and feel the world as she does. A method actor assumes a role and doesn't come out of character until the show closes. If she is playing someone hyper, the actress acts hyper even when she's scrambling eggs in her own kitchen, and sometimes makes a dreadful mess. You'll pretend to be your character until your story is finished. If you have the blues, would it cheer you up to invent a character named Sunny who thinks everything is hunky-dory? It might help your mood, but of course you will have to plunk some problems in Sunny's path to make a good story.

What do you need to know about this character in your story? *Everything!* How do you find out? Once you have a picture of him in your mind, and you know his name, his age, where he lives, if he gets an allowance, it will be as if you have made a new friend.

How do you come to know a real-life friend? What she says and does, the decisions she makes, and her tastes give you clues and information. Finally you will know if you can trust her and where she's weak. Does knowing her family help? How about the way the other kids respond to her, or how she deals with schoolwork? This is the same way you learn about your make-believe character. After you've decided your character not only likes scary movies but they don't even give her bad dreams, you can imagine her exploring an abandoned house, one the other kids think is haunted. Soon you'll understand her so well you'll be able to imagine how she would behave if she had to visit your mother's cranky uncle Henry at the nursing home. Or you'll know how she would reply when snooty Annie Baker is mean to her, as she often is to you.

Have you ever known anyone who seemed perfect? I will bet thirteen trillion dollars he really wasn't. But if he appeared to be, how did you like him? Think of your favorite storybook characters. Do you like and remember the ones who get dirty, rip their jeans, make mistakes, don't always get the guy or the home run, just like you, or the ones who sail to success without hitting any bumps?

Because I know you are serious about writing, I'm going to tell you *the* secret to being a good writer. Save perfectly gorgeous, talented, intelligent, wealthy, noble characters who have families and homes that are a dream come true for your daydreams. Write about real people, the ones with real problems and families who can hurt your feelings and let you down, even when they love you. The stories people admire and respect are the ones that tell it the way it is, not the way we wish it could be.

Physical Appearance

Now let's find your main character, or *protagonist*, which is the literary term for the person who will play the lead in your plot. It's going to be her story. You will invent other characters—friends, family, teachers, mail carriers—but they will play a part only when what they do, say, or think has something to add to your protagonist's tale.

Don't feel boxed in by your age, sex, or species. You can choose as your main character a grandfather, a kangaroo, a hairy monster, or a doll who miraculously comes to life, if you can come to understand why any of them behave as they do.

Start with a physical picture. It's not enough to say she was a beautiful redhead with a terrific figure. Your reader will have to do all the work. Fill in your character's blank face. Decide if she has long legs or knobby knees. That's your job.

Look in the mirror to see how your features make you look different from your cousin Robbie. Study faces on the bus. Look at pictures in magazines. Think of new ways to describe shades of color. How about jay blue or white as a blank sheet of paper?

You probably won't use all the information you'll collect in the exercises below, but it's important for you to have a clear picture of your protagonist. For example, if you decide your character has narrow shoulders and hips like an inflated balloon, you probably won't make him the quarterback of the football team. To make it up to him, you could give him a terrific sense of humor.

When describing a character, don't give every detail

at the same time. You might say, "Now that she was twelve, Cassie wished her body would catch up with her years, but she was still shaped like a Popsicle stick." Later on you could say, "Cassie's bangs needed to be cut. It looked as if a broom were stuck to her forehead." Or "Jamie hated his freckles. Even if all the sappy girls in his sixth-grade class thought they were cute. He might weigh only seventy-five pounds, but he planned to tip the scales at two hundred by the time he tried out for the Knicks. A professional basketball player with freckles was ridiculous. Especially a black basketball player with freckles."

Do the following exercises to help bring your character into focus.

EXERCISES

1. My character is...years old.
2. He/she: is...tall, weighs..., has...colored eyes, and...hair; wears size...shoe, ...jeans, ...dress, ...shirt/blouse. (If your character is an animal, skip the sizes, except perhaps the size of his collar.)
3. My character's best feature is...
4. My character's worst feature is...
5. His nose...
6. Her eyes...(for example, are too big for the rest of her face, sit close to her nose, are squinty and

red because she has allergies, are round as marbles, are slanted and exotic, are heavy-lidded)

7. His skin is...(for example, the color of gingerbread, coffee with double cream, pale as unbleached flour, a Georgia peach, freckled, soft as custard, covered with zits, kissed by the sun)

8. Her hair is...(for example, short, long, nappy, braided, always in her face, shiny in the sun, as many colors as a rainbow cone, in need of a wash, fine as cobwebs, thick as a paint brush, out of control, corkscrew curly, like feathers)

9. Her knees...(for example, have dimples, are covered with scabs, turn in, are bony)

10. His behind...(for example, is flat as a skateboard, wobbles when he runs, fills out his jeans the way the designer intended)

11. Her lips...(for example, are thin and taut, violate her face, are shaped like a heart, are full and sensuous, are too tiny for her long chin)

12. His eyebrows...(for example, grow together, are white, are thick as woolly worms, arch, making him look surprised)

Names

Deciding what to call your character is serious business. Picture him in your mind. Does he look like a

Clarence or a Johnny? Is he the kind of guy who would have a nickname like Tad, short for tadpole? Or if his mother named him William, would no one ever think of calling him Willy? (The French word for nickname is *sobriquet*. Put it in your notebook. You might be able to use it sometime.)

Is your character such a sourpuss that naming her Merry would seem like a bad joke and add humor to your story? Was your character's mother a hippie who named her children after colors, animals, or trees— like Blue, Ivy, and Sycamore? Or was your character given a made-up name like Seaola that embarrasses her? Was she named after some dead hero in her father's native country, or given rich Aunt Matilda's name in hopes she'd be remembered in the will? Was he given the Native American name Riding the Wind, only to be called Joe by the kids at school? Did your character's mother name her after a soap opera star called Taffy, Tanner, Brooke, or Courtney?

How a character feels about his name can also tell a lot about him. When Dannon started junior high school, the coach called him Danny. Even though Dannon wanted desperately to be on the basketball team, he corrected the coach every time: "My name is Dannon." The man still called him Danny, so Dannon stopped answering. It was a matter of principle. Eventually, "Dannon" played forward on that team. You can use the way your protagonist feels about his name to reveal character.

I wish I had a dolphin. If I did I would call him Dickie. My friend named her cat Murphy. I once had a roan horse named Wild Fire. Don't you imagine dogs feel disappointed when their owners call them Spot or Rex?

A president named his daughter Chelsea. I once had a boyfriend named Dallas. You could have some fun with a bold, brassy character named Cheyenne (see page 15).

When I was your age I read two stories no one else ever seems to have heard of, but I still remember them because of the characters' names. One was Meg of Mystery Mountain. I not only liked the alliteration, but Meg rode a horse down the mountain, and I was nuts about horses. The other was a mountain girl too, but her name was Sammie. I still sometimes pretend my name is Sammie.

Do you think your name has affected your personality? If you name your character Priscilla, do you think she will act different from a Billy Sue? If your character just moved to this country from Mexico, would he want to be called Carlos or Charlie? The reason for his choice could make a good story. Would you be more apt to vote for a Pete, a Ralph, or a Beauregard for class president?

Will your character call his father Dad, Pop, Pa, Daddy, Papa, Bill, or the old man—behind his back? Your decision will reveal something about your protagonist.

What about police officers? Will your character refer to them as cops, policemen, the man, pigs, lawmen, patrolmen? The decision will reflect attitude. What if your character's father is a policeman, but her friend calls police officers a disrespectful name such as pigs?

Go back to the section in your notebook where you've been collecting names. If you still haven't found the perfect one for this special character of yours, maybe the following exercises will help. They could work like sourdough starter or yeast for your story. When you have a clear picture of your character and he has a name, he will start telling you what goes on in his life, if you listen.

EXERCISES

1. When you have a son you will name him...
   When you have a daughter you will name her...
   Your favorite doll/teddy was called...
2. You've always dreamed a cool boy would call you, and his name would be...
3. In England boys are sometimes named Evelyn. If

Evelyn moved to the States, what nickname would you have to give him?

4. What if your character's mother liked her maiden name, such as Fitzgerald or Finn, so much she gave it to her child? What are some last names which might work as a first name for your character? Vandemeer is a mouthful, but I like Morgan.

5. Make a list of cities or countries like Paris or India you might name your character.

6. Some people name their children after jewels and precious metals. My mother's name was Pearl, which she didn't like a bit, but I once knew a girl who was proud of being called Ruby. Mick Jagger named his daughter Jade. Other ideas?

7. Think of a nickname that could make your character cry.

8. Your character's pony is known as...because...

9. The best name ever for a goldfish is...

10. If you were writing about a favorite teacher, you would name her... If she were a grouch, you would name her...

11. Southerners often prefer two names, such as John Boy, Kitty Lee, Bobby Joe, Mary Belle, Jim Bob, Betty Lou. Make a list that might work for your characters.

12. Give the following animals names:

- a toad
- a fox
- a bat
- a mean dog
- a worm
- a bucking bronco
- a lamb
- a jumping frog
- a friendly cockroach

Okay, it's time to make that important decision. Take your time. Try to make a choice that will make your story more interesting.

- My character's name will be...because...gave it to her.
- The reason he/she chose the name was...
- She will/will not have a nickname because...
- He will like/hate his name because...

Developing Your Character

Making a new friend can be fun, but not half as much fun as creating a character. Friends can be grumpy, hurt your feelings, be boring, disloyal, moody, or fickle. They can move away. You never know what they are going to do, and usually you can't do anything about the way they behave. But a character? You decide what he does, and you can even tell him what to say. It's a heady experience. You can send him to London or the moon, give her crossed eyes or hair that shimmers to her waist. Your character can be a math whiz, have more boyfriends than your kitchen has ants, write poetry, know how to speak French, look good in a tutu, or have fat thighs. You are in charge.

Most important, you'll never have to be lonely. Creating a character you carry around in your mind is like having a twin, or a best friend who never has to go home. Remember when you had a secret friend when you were a little kid and your brother laughed at you? He can't now. You are a writer, and writers make up people all the time. It's their job.

Once you know your character's name and would recognize her in a crowd, it's time to find out what she's like on the inside. You'll have to know how she feels about everything from baseball to ballet. What does she think about when she can't go to sleep? What does she long for? What things hurt her feelings or embarrass her to death? You can give her some of your interests, add some quirks your cousin has, borrow some fears from a girl you used to know. The idea is to make up a composite (combination) of things to be sure she is an intriguing person. It's okay to have her say things you wish you had the courage to utter. If you are extremely outgoing, it might be interesting to explore how the world would look to a timid girl.

If someone gave your character a hundred dollars, what would she do with it? Would she buy clothes, save it for college, take her family out for dinner, buy a dog, take piano lessons, buy Rollerblades, donate it to the homeless, or order forty-nine gallons of rocky road ice cream? To write a good story you must understand your character as well as you know yourself. Thinking like a writer is a good way to learn about intriguing people you might have missed.

Many immigrant children arrive in this country not speaking or understanding English. Imagine how it feels when they go to a movie. They see the action, but it's as if they're watching a pantomime. At school when other children laugh at a joke, they don't get it. They might even think the laughter is at their expense. You could have your character try to make friends with someone from India, Korea, Cuba, Brazil, Bangladesh, China, Palestine; show how frustrated they become or how they compensate when they don't have language.

Having your character make friends with a young person from a country his family considers enemy territory is another possibility for a good story. (Bette Greene's *Summer of My German Soldier* is a popular novel that explores this theme.) In your story both of the kids might like pizza, video games, dinosaurs, and math, collect major league baseball caps, and not understand why their parents are at odds. How they work it out could make either a funny or a sad story. Think about it. Remember, you get to make all the decisions.

We talked about how boring perfect people can be. You don't want to write about a tiresome character no one will like very much or believe for a second. But you can create someone who is unappealing yet still entertaining. Maybe you already know he has protruding front teeth (*protruding* is a kinder word than *buck* teeth, don't you think?) or bowed legs, but what about his character flaws? Is he scared of the dark? Does he pull the wings off butterflies? Torment little kids? Spend his allowance on foolish things? Hang out with creeps?

After you've decided what weaknesses your character has, you should ask yourself *why* she acts that way. All of us have done things we wish we hadn't. Sometimes guilt makes people do amazing things. They might strut around, hiding their shame behind bravado. Or they could be sorry for their behavior, and their remorse could take away their self-confidence, causing them to be shy with other people. Another guilty person might spend her time trying to please people. These actions are caused by what writers call motivation—the reason for someone's behavior. A baby cries when she's hungry or wet. Her motivation is comfort.

Think about the kids you know well. Some are leaders and some follow the herd. Notice how someone motivated by the need to be in charge acts different from the person who is content to have someone else take the risk, give the speech, make the decision, or do the work.

I'm going to pause here for a moment to discuss process. Usually I like to write more than talk. Seriously. I like writing letters better than speaking on the phone. Ask my mother. I've written her a loooong letter every week since I went away to college. I like the funny, interesting, sometimes lovely things you can make words do. Normally, I enjoy the challenge of making them behave as I wish. But every now and then, I confess it can be frustrating. For example, how do I make young writers understand the importance of knowing what motivates their characters? Decision time. I could put an exclamation point at the end of the sentence. I could put it in italics for emphasis, but I've already used both devices. I could write it in big letters **(MOTIVATION)**, but that makes the page look funny. I could say it is "very," "extremely," "extraordinarily" important, but we've agreed earlier that qualifying a word that already explains what it means (see page 44) weakens the sentence. Perhaps the best I can do is conjure a serious tone, look for convincing and persuasive words, and assume you realize that not only what your character does but why he does it is significant. You're intelligent. You'll get it.

Back to the thesaurus. *Motivation* means drive, impetus, incentive, proclivity, incitement, bent. Okay, so you must know what drives your character's actions, why he does the things he does. His behavior must be consistent. Bullies don't become pussycats without a reason. He can change, but unless a portion of his brain is damaged, he shouldn't take on a different personality and act in a way inconsistent with his temperament as we already know it from earlier incidents in your story.

A worthy antagonist (see page 51) has to be good at her meanness. What motivates her to use her strengths in a bad way? Why does she join a gang rather than the church choir? What weakness does she see in your main character that makes your protagonist vulnerable? Why does she look for that soft spot and poke it? Is she envious? Does she feel she hasn't been treated fairly? Does she want revenge?

Then, some characters just have weird habits and tastes that even a psychiatrist couldn't understand. You've known kids who do the strangest things, like put peanut butter on their ice cream, collect anything purple, make up outlandish stories about people they see on the bus, listen to the same song fifteen times in a row, think horror stories are funny, or won't wear socks, even in the winter. Does your character have any obsessions, tastes, or habits that would raise some eyebrows?

You can give your character weird ideas, too. What if he decides to eat long things like carrots, licorice sticks, or pretzel rods so they'll make him grow tall? How about a character so fascinated by vampires that he paints red teeth marks on his neck?

If you are writing about an animal, you can add humor by working against type. For example, mice are tiny little creatures. You might make yours a tough guy who is not afraid of the biggest tomcat on the block. Chameleons change colors to camouflage themselves for protection. Wouldn't it be a hoot to write about a chameleon who loves pink? He doesn't want to turn green, brown, or blue. He just wants to be pink. You could have him attach himself to a baby's blanket or the good pink towels your protagonist's mother puts out only for company.

You will want not only to know your character but also to understand what kind of home he has. It will affect the way he thinks and behaves. People inherit some of their idiosyncrasies from their families; they also continue to be influenced by what happens at home. I can't imagine parents who don't want to raise healthy, happy kids. Most do a good job. Sure, they have bad days and sometimes lose their tempers, but don't we all? Unfortunately, some criticize so much their kids feel awkward, ugly, or stupid. Others let their little darlings get away with outrageous things. I've even known well-intentioned mothers or fathers who had so little confidence in themselves that they didn't feel as if they should correct their children. Then there are others who screamed and yelled too much because they were frustrated.

Turn on your imagination. Picture your protagonist. Who knows, you might be in the process of inventing a character who will become as well known as Tom Sawyer, Holden Caulfield, Cinderella, or Leslie who built a bridge to Terabithia!

EXERCISES

1. Your character's favorite food is... For breakfast he eats... He wouldn't touch...if someone paid him ten dollars to eat it.
2. Your character's favorites are:
   - book
   - movie and TV star
   - song
   - ice cream flavor
   - relative
   - gemstone

- color
- sport
- outfit
- way to spend Sunday
- pet
- poem
- school subject
- day of the week
- memory
- part of her body
- politician
- place in the neighborhood
- writer
- joke
- shoes
- way to keep warm
- friend
- fantasy

3. The secret your character won't tell anyone is…
4. The one thing he most regrets is…
5. The most embarrassing moment of her life happened when…
6. The thing he is most proud to have done is…
7. The ugliest thing she ever had to wear to school/church/a wedding/a family reunion was…
8. The thing she would like most to change about herself is…
9. The trait most important to him when choosing a friend is…
10. What she likes best about her mother is…
11. In his family he is the baby/oldest/middle child… His position in the family is important because…
12. If he could be reincarnated as an animal, he would come back as a…

13. If he could change anything at home, it would be...
14. ...gives her hope.
15. What people like best about your character is...
16. The best time she ever had in her life was...
17. He most often gets into trouble for...
18. The worst bully she knows is..., who...
19. What scares him the most is...
20. Your character needs more...(for example, courage, friends, money, discipline, integrity, clothes, humor, attention, respect, self-confidence)
21. Your character is afraid of...(for example, being home alone, drug dealers, being laughed at, her brother, flunking, shots [the kind the doctor gives], his monster dreams, the hole in the ozone layer, being embarrassed by his parents, not doing as well as her sister, nothing yet invented)
22. If the school caught on fire, your character would...(for example, faint, stay until everyone else was safe, cry for his mother, run as fast as he could, panic, do exactly what the teacher told him)
23. How would your character react in the following situations:
    • She was accused of something she didn't do.
    • His friend told him a secret your character thought an adult should know.

- A friend said your character would be a "chicken" if she didn't do something she knew was wrong or dangerous.
- Someone tried to make him rat on a friend.
- He saw something under his microscope no one had ever seen.
- She was asked to be the anchor of the Saturday Morning Kids' News.
- Her parents forbade her to see someone she liked a lot.

24. Your character's pet peeve is…
25. If your character has an antagonist, the weak spots his/her enemy can play on are…(for example, he's gullible, she's timid, she's sloppy, he's lazy, he's competitive, she's easily flattered, she's ashamed, she's greedy, she's easily impressed, he's spoiled)

Finding Your Character's Story

When a writer has flushed out an intriguing character, he begins to ask the magic words: *what if?* What if my character ran away from home? What if her sister ran away? What if she began to hang out with tough kids? What if he befriended a kid no one liked? What if she got a horse for her birthday? What if he time- traveled back into history? You envision her in these situations until you say, "Eureka! That's the story I want to tell."

Everyone loves a story that has a dilemma (difficulty, impasse, predicament) in which none of the solutions to a problem are satisfactory. An example might go like this: Pretend your character gets into trouble for something she didn't do. To clear herself she needs only to tell on her best friend, who is guilty. But the friend's parents are known for giving out punishment that exceeds the crime. There's an unpleasant side no matter which decision your character makes. If you understand her personality, you know what she will do, even if it's not the choice you would make in the same situation.

The most boring stories are those that are predictable. You immediately know how they will end, and you can guess how the problems will be solved. A story must be credible (believable), but no one likes to read a tale that has no surprises.

A good writer can make an incredible story seem real if he convinces readers to suspend disbelief. He appeals to their imagination and asks them, for the length of the story, to accept that girls can ride on the backs of eagles, or that gerbils and giraffes can talk, or that boys can time-travel into the future. He creates a world so real it seems plausible (possible, logical). Did you ever doubt for a moment that Peter Pan could fly? Think of the fairy tales you read as a little kid. The gingerbread man ran away, the pigs wore bow ties, the wolf huffed and puffed until he blew their houses down. We believed and enjoyed it all.

Try some of the following exercises (always from the character's point of view) to see if you are inspired.

EXERCISES

1. What if:
   - She and her best friend have always wanted to be actors. Auditions for the lead role in the school play have narrowed down to a final try-

out—between the two of them.

- Martin Luther King called her up. His spirit had come back to town to discuss with her what to do about violence in the schools.
- She and her boyfriend went to acting camp. As director of a play, her boyfriend cast her and his best friend Rob in the leads. He directed them to fall in love, and they did.
- She was accused of stealing, and she had done it.
- He made a discovery in the science lab, but no one would believe him because he was "just a kid."
- Three years after his father died, his mother married a man who had a cool daughter his age.
- Three years after her father died, her mother married a man who had a daughter her age who was a bad seed.
- He won the state science fair, and his prize was to spend the summer working with other science whizzes at the state university. But his father had done his science project. The boy hates science.
- Her younger cousin put her lipstick in the microwave.
- He saw her going to the movies with his best friend.
- Everyone else passed.

- A gang of mean boys held her while the leader hacked off her braid just for the fun of it.
- Her dad said, "It's not your fault, but your mother and I are going to separate."
- The worm in your character's apple said, "Hey, buster, take it easy with those sharp teeth."
- Her boyfriend left a message on her answering machine saying he didn't like her anymore.
- Her dad lost his job.
- In the lunchroom, he squirted mustard all over her. (Consider both characters' point of view.)
- She thought the gym teacher had it in for her.
- Her best friend had a party but didn't invite her.
- She found little purple creatures from outer space in a shoebox in her closet.
- He kissed his date in the backseat of the car, with her father at the wheel.
- Her brother contracted AIDS.

2. Create dilemmas your character could face.
3. Think of unusual combinations of characters you might put together as friends or enemies.
4. Imagine unusual family situations for your character such as:
   - His father teaches in his school. The other kids don't like his father. He does.
   - Her father is the president or a senator. Every-

thing she does is written up in the newspaper, especially the embarrassing things.
- She and her mother are so poor they decide to advertise for a husband and father. Several candidates apply.
- He lives with his bachelor brother, who is twenty-eight and can't cook.
- When her mother dies, she is sent to live with an eccentric aunt who hasn't gone outside her house in the past ten years.

Minor Characters

We will pretend your story is going to be about Chase. You know her personality, her family, how old she is, what she looks like. It's her story, but to tell it, who else will have to appear? A best friend? An enemy? Her pet? A member of her family? A boy? A stranger? What role does this character play in this episode in your protagonist's life? How much does the reader need to know about the minor characters to make the story clear and interesting?

Just as you learned more about your main character than you will probably use in the story, it's also a good idea to probe the personalities of minor characters.

The following questions might help you understand the secondary characters.

EXERCISES

1. If the secondary character is not a family member:
   - Your character has known this person for...(years, weeks, etc.)
   - They met when...
   - He is...years old.
   - She has a good/bad influence on your character.
   - Your character can/cannot trust and rely on him.
   - Her strength is...
   - His weak spot is...
   - An important aspect of her physical appearance is...
   - An important fact about his background is...
   - The relationship between your character and this person will be the same (or have changed) at the end because...
2. If the character is a family member:
   - What is the relationship to your character?
   - He is...years old.
   - How do the other members of your protagonist's family react to her?
   - Is he a sympathetic (you want the reader to like him) or nonsympathetic character?
   - A surprising thing about this person is...

- Is this person responsible for what happens to your character?
- Will this character be critical or supportive of your main character?

3. If the character is an animal:
   - His physical appearance reveals...about his personality.
   - What does your protagonist like best or fear most about this animal?
   - He is a comfort (or a pain in the neck) for your character because...
   - Other people react to her as if...
   - The most unusual thing about him is...
   - Is she the problem or the solution to the conflict in the story?

4. If the character is an antagonist:
   - The root of the problem between them is...
   - The result of your character's winning or losing will be...
   - The antagonist is a worthy opponent because he...(for example, is so clever, seems to have no conscience, understands your character's weaknesses)

There are several ways to make the reader dislike your antagonist. You can describe her unattractive physical traits, give her disgusting habits, show her doing hurtful things to your character, or let the reader know about mean things she has done.

Choosing a Narrator

Close your eyes. Imagine your mother telling a stranger about you. Now imagine your sister or brother talking about you. Picture a friend discussing you. This will hurt, but imagine how someone who doesn't like you would describe you. Are they talking about the same person?

You're drinking your chocolate milk in the cafeteria. Someone bumps into you. Your chocolate milk spews all over the girl behind you. As she tries to wipe the sticky stuff out of her eyes and off her math homework and her new white blouse, she screams that you did it on purpose. The principal appears. Both of you tell what happened. Which story is true?

Do another take. You're watching TV news. The prosecutor coolly describes someone who behaved so inhumanely he is a threat to society. The accused's mother says he's always been a good boy. His neighborhood friend swears this guy wouldn't harm anyone. The accused gives a tearful story, saying he's a victim of the system. Who can you believe?

The same story about the same people changes according to who is telling it. This is called *point of view*. We've discussed it on pages 35–40. Deciding who will be your narrator is one of the most important decisions an author like you has to make.

Jon Scieszka proved the importance of viewpoint when he wrote *The True Story of the Three Little Pigs*. He told it from Al Wolf's perspective. Al swears he was framed. Frankly, I've always wanted to hear Cinderella's stepmother's side of their story. And, if it were possible, wouldn't it be interesting to know if Juliet still thought Romeo was such a cool dude after the whole tragedy was over? He did some stupid things that got both of them killed, for Pete's sake!

You have many choices for your narrator. You can pretend to be your character telling the story in the first person point of view: "My name is Bo Brady. Four years ago, when I was just six, an amazing thing happened to me. I was walking home from school one day when a small airplane landed right in the middle of the street. Would I lie to you?"

Or you as the author can tell the story, from Bo's point of view in the third person. That's like walking through the story in Bo's shoes. You can see, hear, and know only what Bo sees, hears, and knows: "Four years ago, when Bo Brady was only six, an unusual thing happened as he was walking home from school."

A third possibility is to create another character to tell Bo's story (this point of view is called *witness narration*): "A weird thing happened to this buddy of mine about four years ago, when we were only six. Bo—my pal's name is Bo Brady—was bopping along, minding his own business, when..."

In all three cases you have limited your point of view to one person. You can include only what that person sees, hears, says, and thinks and what other people say to him. The advantage of this is a more intimate relationship with the narrator. The reader feels close to him by coming to know how he thinks and feels.

A naive narrator, like a little kid who doesn't understand what he is seeing, can also be effective. A five-year-old describing what his brother does on the football field or how his sister acts toward a boy she likes, or giving his innocent interpretation of what is happening on the street in a bad neighborhood, or stating his firm belief that a monster lives in the basement, can be convincing. The reader will feel intelligent because he knows more than the child.

The other possibility is called the *omniscient viewpoint.* This does not limit you to one person's perspective but allows you to nip into anyone's thoughts and speak from any vantage point. For example, in the Bo Brady story, you could switch to what several characters see and feel. You can tell what the pilot thinks of this kid with a melting Popsicle in his hand who is climbing all over his plane. When a policeman arrives, you could show what he might be thinking: "An airplane in the middle of the street? Terrific. Only on my beat. If this kid had only waited ten minutes to call, my shift would've been over and I could've been at the Yankee game."

Before you decide who will tell your story, imagine how the story will change if seen from the different viewpoints. Try some of the following warm-up exercises.

EXERCISES

1. Your character's parents tell him they are going to get a divorce. Tell it from the point of view of the parent who wants the divorce. Retell it from the point of view of the one who does not.
2. Your character is taking her cat with her on a plane trip to visit her grandparents. The cat won't get in the carrier. Give the cat's point of view. Rewrite it from the girl's viewpoint.
3. Judy Blume or another famous writer comes to talk to your class. Write the scene from an omniscient point of view, zooming into several kids' reactions. Then revise it, telling it from the author's vantage point.

4. A timid ghost tries to make friends with some kids playing in their backyard after dark. Have the ghost tell the story. Imagine how differently the children would relate the incident.

5. The family parks in a lot. A man with a gun demands the father's wallet. The three-year-old thinks it is a cap pistol. Tell the story from the child's viewpoint. Retell it from the robber's point of view.

6. Kim and Karen are thirteen-year-old twins. They go shopping for winter coats. Their mother and Kim want the coats to be identical. Karen wants to be an individual. Give Karen's perspective, then the mother's.

7. In the following situations, which point of view would be most effective—first person, third person, omniscient, or a naive narrator?
   * At the zoo, a chimp escapes from his cage, jumps over the fence, and lands on the back of a zebra.
   * John and Jerry played baseball for Central. John moves to the Lincoln school district. Lincoln's first game is against Central.
   * Jessie, ten years old, is the first girl pitcher on the Little League team. The local TV station asks her to come in to be interviewed by Candy Cotton. Jessie is so nervous that when the camera starts to roll, she throws up on Candy.

- Percival is the only inhabitant in the tropical fish tank. Then someone pours ten strange-looking creatures into his water.
- A class and their teacher take the train into the city to go to the museum. While going through a narrow tunnel the train gets stuck.
- Alice saves her money until she has just enough to take Virginia, a girl she wants to be her friend, for a soda. Virginia brings her cousin Heather. Neither of them are carrying a wallet.

8. Look at your favorite book to see from whose viewpoint the story is told. Write another chapter from a different point of view.

9. Find an item in the newspaper. Tell the story as someone in the story would tell it.

10. Following Jon Scieszka's lead, rewrite a fairy tale from a different character's point of view.

Describing the Setting

Do you want your character to live on Venus, in Vancouver, or in a van? It's your decision. I told you being a writer was a lot of fun.

The setting is the physical, and sometimes spiritual, background where the story takes place. It's more than simply the geographical location, though. And it's not just the scenery or where the furniture, doors, and windows are located. It's the atmosphere. Is it bleak or gay, cold or friendly, familiar or foreign? Time is another aspect of the setting. Does the story take place in the future, the present, or the past? The season of the year and the time of day can also be important.

Describing where the story takes place can be as important as creating a picture of your characters. Let's pretend your story will take place one afternoon on a vacant lot in a poor city neighborhood. Picture the scene. What details will bring it alive? The mesh fence? Litter? The foundation of an old building? Is the fence rusty or new? Has it been bent so someone can crawl through? If that is a morning glory climbing on the old foundation it must be summer. Is there a soggy teddy bear lying under that pile of pop cans and fast-food containers? What sounds do you hear? Can you smell the flower or something rotten in the litter? Do you see stores, apartment buildings, or houses across the street?

Maybe your story takes place in your character's bedroom. Does she share it, or is this her private place? Did she or her mother decorate it? Is she neat or messy? How can you show rather than tell what time it is? A clock could strike four, but unless we know she just came home from school or you've explained how dark it is, we won't know if it is early morning or late afternoon. How might you show her interests by describing what is in the room? Are those ballet slippers or spikes in the corner? Does she have a computer or a boom box? Are the pictures on her bulletin board of horses or boys?

If you said, "Jason passed the Empire State Building on his way to Central Park," is there any reason to add that he lives in Manhattan? But even if you have your character swim in Lake Michigan, you'd better explain that he lives in Chicago, because there are other cities on the lake. Sometimes naming the actual city or state isn't important. Maybe the story you're telling could have taken place in any big city where the streets are crowded, or on any farm where they grow corn higher than your character's head. Don't stick in a location unless it serves a purpose.

Imagine a story that happened before the Civil War. How do you let your reader know immediately you've moved back into another century? You might say, "Abraham Lincoln hadn't even begun to practice law when Samantha's father moved the family to a little town on the Illinois side of the Mississippi." Or, "In another ten years Abel and Seth would be fighting on different sides in the Civil War, but that summer they were best pals."

If your story takes place in an alien environment, you will need to give many details to create the picture. Maybe the food tastes like peppermint and all the plants are pink or red. It could be fun to imagine a place that lacks gravity—so your characters waft through the air, balls don't bounce, and Mom never breaks a dish.

However, don't get carried away describing things like the sun shining through a stained-glass window, or the potholes in the street, unless the details are relevant to developing your character, moving the plot along, or creating an atmosphere or mood important to the story.

Think, too, about the time frame of your story. How much time passes from the beginning to the end—a few minutes, two years, a week? I realize you are a very interesting person, but can you imagine how tedious a story would be that began: "Mom woke me at seven A.M. My first thought was about the essay I forgot to write. I pulled the cover over my head. Mom pulled it off. I stretched..." Ho-hum. If you included every detail, you'd have a hundred pages by the time you made it to the breakfast table, and you still wouldn't be anywhere near the action of the story: soccer practice after school.

Flashback is a literary term you'll need to understand when structuring your story's time sequence. Since it's not possible to include everything that happened in your character's life, you've picked one day or one week for the action. But things important to the story happened before the tale opens. Writers and actors call these events the *backstory*. You provide that information by using flashbacks, a technique that works just as it sounds: It takes you back to an earlier period. For example, if your character's mother tells her about something that happened when she was a baby, she is flashing back in time. You will need to write a *transi-*

tion, which might go like this: "When you were two years old, one day I took you to the circus. Back then I had no idea you would want to be a clown when you grew up." Or you might say: "Before I was even old enough to talk, my mother took me to the circus, and…" If you remember to create a sense of time and place, you can flash back smoothly.

To move from one setting to another, as well as from one time period to another, a writer also uses transitions. For example: "I knew when I woke up this morning, it was going to be a bad day. I had forgotten to write my essay. *By the time soccer practice started after school*, I wasn't even surprised when the coach said he was cutting me from the team." In that instance you skipped several hours. You can move ahead even faster in years: "That afternoon when I was cut from the soccer team, I thought my life was over. *Now, twenty-five years later*, as I watch my daughter play, I am glad it wasn't."

You can skip time, even move from Minneapolis to the moon, as long as you remember to take the reader with you. To follow your story, she must always have a sense of place and time. "I kissed my cat, kicked my brother, and went to see Marsha. The refrigerator at Marsha's house looked like a storehouse for squirrels. Her mother was on a diet." Because nothing interesting happened to the character as she walked to her friend's house, leave the walk out. But remember to tell the reader where the next scene is taking place.

The following exercises should help you to think about a sense of place and time for your story.

EXERCISES

1. My story opens: time...day of the week...season of the year...
2. At the end,...time has passed.
3. The time/day/season is important because...
4. An unusual atmosphere is important. Describe a tense setting, a scary one, and an exciting one.
5. My story takes place in...(town, city, state, village, farm, country, planet). The primary action happens in the following locations...
6. Write transitions for the following situations:
   - On Monday John asks Sarah to the dance. In the next scene it is Friday night, the night of the dance.
   - Your character moves from the ball game to the locker room, or he moves from the locker room into the car going home.
   - Sadie boards the spaceship in Cleveland. She arrives on Pluto.
   - Your character is in a marvelous mood. Something happens. He is down in the dumps.

7. Add details to make the following settings as clear as a scene in a movie. This is the place to use the observations you've been putting in your notebook. Don't forget odors:
   - a P.E. class
   - a fish tank
   - the backseat of a car
   - the first day of school
   - a carnival
   - a two-year-old's birthday party
   - a rabbit hole
   - a dugout
   - a museum
   - an alien land
   - a sleeping bag on a cold night
   - backstage
   - a deli
   - an orchestra pit
   - a parade
   - the ocean
   - a slumber party
   - Mom's office
   - Dad's garage
   - an uncomfortable chair
   - a supermarket
   - a pasture
   - a stable

Structuring Your Story

Think how much you have accomplished. You have a protagonist with a story you want to tell, and some minor characters. You have made the important decisions about who will tell the tale, where it will take place, and how much time it will cover. You can feel proud.

Your next step is to structure the material. Think of your idea as a lump of clay. Stories have to be shaped into three parts: the beginning, middle, and end. In the beginning, you introduce your character, show the point of view and the setting, and give readers a hint as to what the story will be about. In the middle, things happen to complicate the situation. It's where your character tries to solve the problem, find a way over the hurdles, and accomplish a goal. In the end, your character wins, loses, gives up, or finds a way to live with the problem. The ending or conclusion explains the results of her winning, losing, giving up, or finding a way to live with it.

If you are as good at this as I think you are, your character will probably have learned something about her nature she hadn't known before. She will be different than she was in the beginning—wiser, sadder, happier, friendlier, more mature.

For example, say a story opens with Gillian troubled because her mother refuses to talk about the father Gillian has never seen. Gillian is a very determined, intelligent, and curious girl. She sets out to solve the mystery. By snooping in her mother's private papers, she learns she is a test-tube baby. Her mother has no idea who her father is. The conclusion shows how Gillian handles the realization that she will never be able to know her father. It also shows how she feels about her mother's decision to have a child in this way.

Stories are about cause and effect. Something happens (a cause); what results is the effect.

Cause: When Gillian has to fill out a paper at school that asks for her father's name, she decides to solve the mystery.

Effect: After learning she is a test-tube baby, she is proud of her mother's courage, or...

Effect: She is so embarrassed she makes up a story about her father's death, or...

Effect: She turns against her mother for concealing the truth.

Now That You Are a Writer, You Should Know These Literary Terms

Language is essential no matter what career you choose. Most professions have particular terms you must learn. It can be like speaking in code. Doctors have the hardest job. They not only have to know what streptococcus means, but also how to spell it. I thought someone was kidding me the first time I learned how pneumonia was spelled. When computer experts talk about bytes, it isn't dangerous, unless they get carried away making puns. Now that you are a writer, you should understand literary language, the tools of your trade, such as:

Exposition: You don't actually say "once upon a time," but that is really how all stories begin. M. E. Kerr says she doesn't begin to write until she knows her story so well she is eager to tell someone about it. She sits down at her typewriter, thinks about an audience, and says, "Wait till you hear this."

The exposition is the beginning of the story that creates the tone, gives the setting, introduces the characters, and supplies facts necessary to understand the story. If your character shaves his head and his appearance is important, describe his bald head immediately, or the reader may create a picture of him with thick, curly locks. If your beaver has no tail, let the reader know from the start he's handicapped. A story taking place on Mars or in the future should not keep the location or time a secret for long, or it will confuse the reader.

Ask yourself what facts must be communicated immediately in your story. Is your protagonist poor? Do his parents ride the rodeo? Did her favorite sister die before the story opens? Is a tornado predicted for this very night? Have all of her friends been kissed and she hasn't? Is he the smallest whale in the pod? Facts essential to understand your story should appear in the exposition.

The story is a series of incidents that make up the action. In a story, you ask "and then what happened?" The plot explains *why* these things happen. E. M. Forster said it best: The king died, and then the queen died, is the story. The king died, and then the queen died of a broken heart, is the plot.

You begin to set up the plot immediately. You can let the reader know on the first page there is trouble (conflict) or a problem to solve. The challenge is to create doubts in the reader's mind or arouse his suspicion so he wants to read on to find out what happens next. Conflicts are those big, small, funny, or serious things that cause dreams not to come true or things not to turn out as hoped. For example, your character drops her bus ticket down a grate, or he sneezes when he starts to kiss her for the first time. Problems can arise because of the weather, trouble with people, school grades, natural enemies. Gillian's conflict is not knowing who her father is; McGuire the Scottie has fleas and his owner hasn't even noticed.

Rising action, complication, or middle: You've introduced your character, described the setting, and established the problem to be solved or the goal to be reached. Now complications begin to arise, creating suspense and tension. The reader will want to know what is going to happen next and how the story is going to end. Gillian finds the box where her mother keeps important papers. It is locked. She hears her mother's footsteps on the stairs. Or McGuire's owner is about to pet him. The Scottie raises his leg to scratch hard. The phone rings.

The rising actions are things that create tension, mounting to a point where something must happen: Gillian finds the papers or gives up; McGuire gets some relief or strikes out on his own to find the vet. This high point in the story is the *climax*. Something happens that changes the situation or your character: Gillian breaks the lock on the box; McGuire gets lost and a little boy finds him. But the story isn't over yet. As a result of the action rising to a climax, how do things turn out?

Conclusion, denouement, falling action, or end: How your character handles or reacts to the events at the climax of your story will determine how the story ends. In some yarns the reader may only come to know the true nature of your character when he sees how she responds to the climax. What follows that high point is called the falling action, where you unravel the plot and explain the outcome. In the denouement, a synonym for the conclusion, you explain any secrets or misunderstandings and answer the questions you've raised about the plot or the character.

Perhaps Gillian's mother explains that she had loved someone when she was young, but it hadn't worked out. After that she never met anyone she wanted to spend her life with, but she wanted a child more than anything. Gillian understands how much her mother wanted her, and feels good, or perhaps she decides her mother was selfish. I don't know about McGuire— you'll have to figure out what happens to him and his fleas.

In the best stories, the end is only the beginning. For example, if your character is twelve years old, she will probably go on to high school, college, get married, have children. If you have been able to make her seem like a real person, the reader can imagine not only things that might happen to her the day after the story ends or ten years later, but predict how she would respond. Good characters live on in the reader's imagination.

EXERCISES

1. In the exposition, I will introduce my character by...
2. I will show the setting by...
3. I will present the conflict that must be resolved by...
4. Incidents from the backstory that I will flash back to are:
5. The complications that will make the story interesting are:
6. The climax of my story will be when...
7. What happens as a result of the climax will be...
8. In the end my character will have...(for example, solved the problem, reached his goal, resolved the conflict, lost his battle, given up)

Writing Activities to Do with a Friend

Form a Writers' Group

Writers often meet to discuss their work. Three groups meet at my house to read the stories we are working on. We give and receive feedback, and we always begin by doing warm-up exercises like the ones in this book. You could use these or make up your own.

You and your friends could meet at each other's houses on Saturday afternoon or after school to share what you've written. It's a good idea to begin by saying what you liked about your friends' work. Then if there was something you didn't understand or a part that wasn't clear, your questions or criticism will be easier for them to handle.

Write with Your Friends

Practicing writing can be fun if you do it with others. Pick a topic—a silly one like bubble gum, or a scary one like violence. Some of the following might be fun:

- dreadful dreams you've had
- The world could be better if…
- School could be better if…
- Home could be better if…
- I could be better if…
- If I had one wish…
- jerks
- jocks
- gossips
- show-offs
- snobs
- earth angels

Write your own thoughts for ten minutes or so. Then each group member takes a turn reading his or her work. You'll understand how different points of view can be.

Rewrite a Well-Known Story

Pick a well-known story or a fairy tale. Write a wacky new ending, add a character, or change a recognizable one's disposition.

Write a TV Show Episode

Pretend you're writing next week's plot for your favorite sitcom. Discuss ideas. Write one episode as a group project with everyone contributing.

Bind and Illustrate Your Story

After you've worked hard on a story, make it look professional. Use construction paper or a folder for the jacket. Print the title and author's name. If someone else does illustrations, give him credit. Write flap copy, hinting about the plot without giving away any surprises. Put your picture on the back with a short biographical sketch.

If someone in your writers' group said something quotable, such as your story made her laugh for days, include her words and name on the back also. Be sure to have a dedication page. Think how proud the person to whom you dedicate your book will be.

Hold a book fair and invite guests to see and read your work.

Whether you work alone or in a group, the most important thing is to think like a writer. Remember, everything is material. Don't leave home without your notebook. Now that you've trained your eyes, nose, and ears not to miss anything, you are bound to have more adventures; be sure to write them down. You learn to write by writing. Trust me.

Have fun.

index

Lou Willett Stanek wrote a column, "Lou's Teen Talk," for her hometown newspaper when she was thirteen. With a little time off for adventures such as training horses, flying as a stewardess, and lecturing on a cruise ship, she has been writing or teaching ever since. Her junior high school, high school, college, and graduate students have given her many ideas. She is grateful.

Dr. Stanek has written three novels for young adults, *Megan's Beat*, *Gleanings*, and *Katy Did*, along with two nonfiction works for adults, *Whole Language: Literature, Learning, and Literacy* and *So You Want to Write a Novel*. A frequent contributor to magazines and newspapers, she was the 1993 gold medal winner of Cahner's Medal of Excellence.

Stanek earned her Ph.D. at the University of Chicago, M.A. at Northwestern University, and B.A. at Eastern Illinois University. She has served as a trustee at Milliken University. A Midwesterner, she now lives in New York City and teaches writing at The New School for Social Research.